Unwinding Brexit

Pathways to Rejoining the EU

A Short Introduction by K.R. Stonebridge

Unwinding Brexit:
Pathways to Rejoining the EU

ISBN: 9798873151394

Printed in the United States of America

Contents

Chapter 2:
The Case for Reversal

Chapter 3:
Legal and Political Mechanisms

Chapter 4:
Public Opinion and Political Will

Chapter 5:
Economic Implications

Chapter 6:
Diplomatic Dynamics

Introduction

Overview of Brexit: Background and Current Status

Brexit, a portmanteau of "British exit," refers to the United Kingdom's decision to leave the European Union (EU), a political and economic union of 27 European countries. This unprecedented move marked a significant shift in European politics and has had far-reaching implications for both the UK and the EU.

The Genesis of Brexit

The roots of Brexit can be traced back to a growing euro-skepticism in the UK, a sentiment fueled by concerns over sovereignty, immigration, and the perceived bureaucratic nature of the EU. In 2013, then Prime Minister David Cameron, facing pressure from within his own Conservative Party and the rising popularity of the UK Independence Party (UKIP), promised a referendum on the UK's membership in the EU. This pledge was actualized on June 23, 2016, when the UK held a referendum in which 52% of voters opted to leave the EU.

The Referendum Aftermath

The referendum result sent shockwaves throughout the world. It led to the resignation of Cameron and the ascension of Theresa May as Prime Minister. May's tenure was largely defined by negotiations with the EU and attempts to craft a Brexit deal that would be acceptable to both the EU and the divided UK Parliament. These efforts were marred by significant challenges, including disagreements over the Irish border and the rights of EU citizens in the UK and vice versa.

The Transition to Boris Johnson

With May's failure to secure Parliamentary approval for her Brexit deal, Boris Johnson took over as Prime Minister in July 2019.

Johnson, a vocal supporter of Brexit, renegotiated the withdrawal agreement with the EU, particularly around the contentious Northern Ireland protocol. Despite numerous political obstacles, the revised deal was finally approved by the UK Parliament.

The Official Exit and Transition Period

The UK officially left the EU on January 31, 2020. This was followed by a transition period, lasting until December 31, 2020, during which the UK continued to follow EU rules while both parties negotiated their future relationship. These negotiations were complex, focusing on trade, security, and fishing rights, among other issues.

The Trade Deal and Its Implications

A trade deal, known as the Trade and Cooperation Agreement, was eventually reached on December 24, 2020, just days before the transition period ended. This eleventh-hour agreement outlined the new economic and social relationship between the UK and the EU. It allowed tariff-free and quota-free trade in goods but did not prevent new customs checks and regulatory hurdles, which have since impacted businesses and consumers.

Current Status and Ongoing Issues

As of now, Brexit continues to impact various sectors. Trade between the UK and EU has faced disruptions due to new non-tariff barriers. The financial services sector, a crucial part of the UK economy, has lost some of its passporting rights, which allowed unfettered access to EU markets. Furthermore, the Northern Ireland protocol remains a contentious issue, with ongoing debates over its implementation and its impact on the delicate political balance in Northern Ireland.

The Societal Impact

Beyond economics, Brexit has had a profound societal impact. It has altered the landscape of UK politics, leading to changes in party leadership and a realignment of political priorities. The decision to leave the EU has also sparked discussions about the future of the United Kingdom, particularly in Scotland, where calls for another independence referendum have gained traction, partly due to the desire to rejoin the EU.

The Global Perspective

Internationally, Brexit has changed the dynamics of the EU and has had implications for global trade and diplomacy. The EU has lost one of its largest members and a significant diplomatic and military power, leading to shifts in its internal power structure. For the UK, Brexit has meant the pursuit of new trade deals and partnerships beyond Europe, reflecting a shift in its foreign policy focus.

Conclusion

In conclusion, Brexit represents a complex and multifaceted shift in both UK and European politics. Its full implications are still unfolding, and its long-term impact remains to be seen. The UK and the EU continue to navigate this new relationship, addressing ongoing challenges and adapting to a changing global landscape. As such, Brexit remains a pivotal event in early 21st-century history, with lessons and consequences that will be studied for years to come.

Purpose and Scope of the Book

The decision of the United Kingdom to leave the European Union, popularly known as Brexit, stands as one of the most significant political events in recent history. Its ramifications, both anticipated and unforeseen, continue to ripple across the UK, Europe, and the broader international community. This book aims to delve into the intricate tapestry of Brexit, not just as a historical event, but as an ongoing narrative with evolving implications. Our purpose is to offer a comprehensive exploration of the potential pathways and ramifications of a hypothetical reversal of Brexit.

Defining the Purpose

The primary purpose of this book is to provide a detailed, multidisciplinary analysis of the possibility of reversing Brexit. It seeks to examine this scenario from various angles including legal, economic, political, and social perspectives. The book does not advocate for or against the reversal of Brexit; instead, it aims to present an unbiased, thorough investigation of what such a reversal could entail. By doing so, it intends to inform readers, spark dialogue, and contribute to the understanding of this complex and contentious topic.

Scope of the Book

Legal Analysis

A significant portion of the book is dedicated to dissecting the legal frameworks that would come into play should a reversal be considered. This includes an examination of both domestic UK law and EU treaties and regulations. The book will explore the legal precedents, processes, and challenges inherent in such an unprecedented move.

Economic Perspectives

The economic implications of both Brexit and its potential reversal are vast and complex. This book will analyze the economic impact of Brexit thus far and project the potential economic outcomes of rejoining the EU. This includes a study of trade, market access, regulatory alignments, and the broader economic strategies of the UK post-Brexit.

Political Dynamics

Understanding the political landscape is crucial in assessing the feasibility of reversing Brexit. The book will explore the political will, both in the UK and within the EU, for such a reversal. This includes an analysis of public opinion, party politics, leadership roles, and the broader geopolitical context.

Social and Cultural Considerations

Brexit is not just a political and economic event; it has deep social and cultural implications. The book will delve into the societal impact of Brexit, examining issues such as national identity, immigration, and the cultural ties between the UK and Europe. It will also consider how these factors might influence or be influenced by a potential reversal.

Case Studies and International Comparisons

To provide context and depth, the book will include case studies of other major political reversals and re-alignments in history. It will also draw comparisons with similar international situations, offering insights into the challenges and successes of comparable events.

Future Scenarios

Finally, the book will venture into speculative territory, exploring various scenarios that could unfold if Brexit were to be reversed. This includes short-term and long-term projections, considering different political, economic, and social variables.

Intended Audience

This book is designed for a wide range of readers. It is intended to be accessible to those with little prior knowledge of Brexit, while also providing depth and insight for those more familiar with the subject. This includes students, academics, policymakers, business leaders, and anyone interested in contemporary political affairs.

Conclusion

In essence, this book seeks to provide a balanced exploration of what reversing Brexit could mean for the UK, the EU, and the wider world. It aspires to be a comprehensive resource, illuminating the myriad facets of this complex and evolving issue. Through this exploration, the book aims not only to educate and inform but also to foster a deeper understanding of the broader implications of such significant political decisions.

Chapter 1: The Brexit Journey

Detailed History from the Referendum to the Final Exit

The journey of Brexit, from its inception as a referendum to its final execution, encapsulates a tumultuous period in British and European history. This chapter provides a detailed narrative of the events, decisions, and dynamics that shaped the path of the United Kingdom's departure from the European Union.

The Inception: The Referendum Call

The story of Brexit begins with Prime Minister David Cameron's strategic decision in 2013 to promise a referendum on the UK's membership in the EU. This was partly a response to internal pressures within the Conservative Party and the rising challenge from the UK Independence Party (UKIP), advocating for a departure from the EU. The referendum, held on June 23, 2016, resulted in a narrow yet decisive victory for the Leave campaign, with 52% voting to exit the EU.

The Immediate Aftermath and Political Turbulence

The referendum result was a shock to many, triggering immediate political and economic reactions. David Cameron, having campaigned for Remain, resigned as Prime Minister, leading to Theresa May's appointment. Her tenure was defined by the struggle to form a Brexit strategy that would be agreeable to both the EU and the divided factions within her own party. The period was marked by intense negotiations and political strife, including significant parliamentary debates and votes on the nature of the UK's departure.

The Brexit Negotiations

Theresa May's government focused on negotiating a withdrawal agreement with the EU. These negotiations were complex and fraught with challenges, particularly around the issues of the financial settlement, the rights of EU citizens in the UK and vice versa, and the border between Northern Ireland and the Republic of Ireland. The Irish border issue, in particular, proved to be a significant stumbling block, given the need to avoid a hard border due to the Good Friday Agreement.

The Withdrawal Agreement and Political Deadlock

After lengthy negotiations, May's government reached a withdrawal agreement with the EU in November 2018. However, the agreement faced severe opposition in the UK Parliament, particularly over the 'backstop' provision designed to prevent a hard border in Ireland. The deal was rejected three times by Parliament, leading to a political deadlock and necessitating extensions of the Brexit deadline.

Leadership Change and a New Approach

In July 2019, Boris Johnson succeeded Theresa May as Prime Minister, bringing a more hardline approach to Brexit. He renegotiated parts of the withdrawal agreement, particularly the Northern Ireland protocol, and took a firmer stance on the October 31 deadline. Johnson's government then called a snap general election in December 2019, which resulted in a significant majority for the Conservative Party, effectively breaking the parliamentary deadlock.

Finalizing Brexit

With a strong parliamentary majority, Boris Johnson was able to get the revised withdrawal agreement approved by the UK Parliament. The UK formally left the EU on January 31, 2020, entering a transition period that lasted until December 31, 2020. During this time, the UK continued to follow EU rules while the future relationship, particularly regarding trade, was negotiated.

The Trade and Cooperation Agreement

Negotiations for a post-Brexit trade deal were intense and went down to the wire, with a deal – the Trade and Cooperation Agreement – finally being agreed upon on December 24, 2020. This agreement set out the terms of the future UK-EU relationship, including provisions on trade, law enforcement, and dispute resolution, but did not cover services, a significant part of the UK's economy.

The Conclusion of the Transition Period

The transition period concluded on December 31, 2020, marking the end of the UK's participation in the EU Single Market and Customs Union. This marked the first time in history that a major country had left a major trading bloc, setting a new course for the UK's national and international identity.

Reflecting on the Brexit Journey

The journey of Brexit was marked by intense political debate, legal challenges, and economic uncertainty. It was a journey that reshaped the UK's political landscape, redefined its relationship with Europe, and had profound implications for the future of the EU itself. As the UK embarked on its post-Brexit path, the full impact of these changes continued to unfold, forming a crucial chapter in the early 21st-century geopolitical narrative.

Political, Economic, and Social Impacts of Brexit on the UK and EU

The decision by the United Kingdom to leave the European Union, known as Brexit, has had profound political, economic, and social impacts both within the UK and across the EU. This section explores these multifaceted effects, offering a comprehensive view of the aftermath of this significant geopolitical event.

Political Impacts

On the United Kingdom

Brexit has dramatically altered the political landscape of the UK. The Conservative Party, traditionally seen as a party of stability and economic pragmatism, became increasingly divided over the issue. This division led to a change in party leadership and a shift in the party's ideological stance. On the other side, the Labour Party faced its challenges, struggling to articulate a clear position on Brexit amid a membership divided between Leave and Remain supporters.

Moreover, Brexit has intensified discussions on Scottish independence and Irish unification. Scotland, which voted overwhelmingly to remain in the EU, has reignited calls for another referendum on independence, seeing Brexit as a material change in circumstances since the 2014 vote. Similarly, in Northern Ireland, the Brexit process and the implementation of the Northern Ireland Protocol have fueled debates about the future of the union.

On the European Union

For the EU, Brexit marked the first time a member state chose to leave the union, challenging the notion of EU membership as a perpetual commitment. It spurred introspection and debates on the future direction of the union, its policies, and its governance structures. Additionally, Brexit led to a realignment of power within the EU, with France and Germany emerging as even more central to EU decision-making.

Economic Impacts

On the United Kingdom

Economically, Brexit has had significant repercussions for the UK. The uncertainty surrounding Brexit negotiations and the future UK-EU relationship led to volatility in financial markets and a depreciation of the pound. Businesses faced challenges due to uncertainty about future trade arrangements, impacting investment decisions.

Post-Brexit, the UK has experienced disruptions in trade with the EU, its largest trading partner. New non-tariff barriers, customs checks, and regulatory divergences have increased costs and complexity for businesses. Industries that heavily rely on just-in-time supply chains, like automotive and pharmaceuticals, have been particularly affected. Moreover, the services sector, a vital part of the UK economy, faces uncertainty as the Trade and Cooperation Agreement largely omits services.

On the European Union

The EU also felt the economic impacts of Brexit, though its larger and more diversified economy cushioned the blow. Regions and industries with close ties to the UK, such as the automotive sector in Germany and the agri-food sector in Ireland, faced specific challenges. The loss of the UK's financial contribution to the EU budget also necessitated adjustments in EU funding and priorities.

Social Impacts

On the United Kingdom

Socially, Brexit has highlighted and exacerbated divisions within British society. The referendum and subsequent debates have underscored divisions along lines of geography, age, education, and socio-economic status. This polarization has manifested in a more fragmented society, with increased reports of xenophobia and racial intolerance.

Brexit has also affected the lives of EU citizens in the UK and UK citizens living in the EU. Uncertainties about their rights, status, and future have caused significant distress and disruption, impacting community dynamics and individual life choices.

On the European Union

In the EU, Brexit has stimulated discussions on European identity, solidarity, and the future of the European project. It has also led to a surge in support for the EU in some member states, as citizens reflect on the benefits of EU membership.

Conclusion

In conclusion, Brexit has had extensive political, economic, and social impacts on both the UK and the EU. Politically, it has reshaped party politics and national debates in the UK and led to a power shift within the EU. Economically, it has introduced new challenges and uncertainties, particularly in terms of trade and investment. Socially, it has exposed and deepened societal divisions and raised questions about identity and community. As the UK and EU continue to adapt to their new relationship, the full extent of these impacts will unfold over the coming years, shaping the future of both the UK and Europe.

Chapter 2:
The Case for Reversal

Arguments and Motivations for Considering a Reversal

The debate over the reversal of Brexit, while speculative, hinges on a range of arguments and motivations stemming from economic, political, social, and strategic considerations. This chapter delves into the various reasons why some factions in the UK and EU have advocated or contemplated the idea of reversing Brexit.

Economic Arguments for Reversal

Trade and Economic Stability

One of the foremost arguments for reversing Brexit concerns the economic implications of leaving the EU. The departure has led to disruptions in trade, increased costs, and complexities for businesses engaging in cross-border trade. Rejoining the EU could potentially restore the benefits of the Single Market and Customs Union, ensuring tariff-free trade and smoother supply chains.

Financial Services and Investment

The UK's financial services sector, a cornerstone of its economy, has lost seamless access to the EU market. Reversal proponents argue that rejoining would regain the passporting rights crucial for the industry. Additionally, the uncertainty around Brexit has impacted investment flows into the UK. A reversal could bolster investor confidence by providing a more stable and predictable business environment.

Political Arguments for Reversal

Unity and National Cohesion

Brexit has exacerbated political divisions within the UK, notably in Scotland and Northern Ireland. Reversal advocates suggest that rejoining the EU could help alleviate these tensions and contribute to national cohesion, particularly if the decision is backed by a clear democratic mandate.

Global Influence and Diplomacy

As a member of the EU, the UK played a significant role in shaping EU policies. Leaving the EU has diminished the UK's influence in European and global affairs. Proponents of reversal argue that rejoining would restore the UK's voice and influence in the EU, thus strengthening its position on the global stage.

Social Arguments for Reversal

Protecting Citizens' Rights

The post-Brexit landscape has raised concerns about the rights and status of EU citizens in the UK and vice versa. Rejoining the EU could resolve these uncertainties, ensuring freedom of movement and the associated rights for citizens.

Cultural and Educational Benefits

EU membership offers cultural and educational benefits, including participation in programs like Erasmus+. Advocates for reversal highlight the value of these programs in fostering cultural exchange and educational opportunities, which have been curtailed since Brexit.

Strategic Motivations for Reversal

Responding to Changing Public Opinion

If public opinion shifts significantly against Brexit, particularly in light of its practical impacts, this could be a compelling reason for considering a reversal. The democratic legitimacy of such a move would hinge on the clear and expressed will of the people.

Long-Term Economic and Strategic Planning

Some arguments for reversal are based on long-term strategic planning. The interconnected nature of global challenges, such as climate change and international security, requires close collaboration with neighboring countries. EU membership could be seen as strategically beneficial in addressing these challenges collectively.

Conclusion

In conclusion, the case for considering the reversal of Brexit is built on a foundation of economic, political, social, and strategic arguments. These arguments encapsulate the desire for economic stability, political unity, social well-being, and strategic foresight. While the feasibility and likelihood of such a reversal are subjects of debate, understanding these motivations is crucial for any comprehensive discussion on the future relationship between the UK and the EU.

Analysis of the Economic, Political, and Social Benefits of Rejoining the EU

Rejoining the European Union, a scenario contemplated by some in the aftermath of Brexit, presents a range of potential economic, political, and social benefits. This section analyzes these benefits, offering insights into how reintegration with the EU could positively impact the United Kingdom.

Economic Benefits

Enhanced Trade Opportunities

A pivotal benefit of rejoining the EU would be the restoration of frictionless trade. The EU's Single Market and Customs Union facilitate the free movement of goods, services, capital, and labor, which can significantly boost trade efficiency and reduce costs for businesses. For the UK, this means smoother supply chains, lower trade barriers, and potentially increased exports to EU markets.

Economic Stability and Growth

EU membership provides a framework for economic stability, offering access to a large consumer market and a platform for international trade agreements. The predictability and security offered by this framework can stimulate investment and economic growth. Additionally, the UK would likely see a return of financial services to London, reinstating its status as a leading global financial hub.

Agricultural and Fisheries Support

The EU's Common Agricultural Policy (CAP) and fisheries agreements offer support and subsidies to these sectors. Rejoining could provide British farmers and fishermen with financial aid and market access, crucial for the sustainability of these industries.

Political Benefits

Reinforced International Influence

EU membership amplifies the UK's voice in international affairs. As part of the EU, the UK would regain its ability to influence EU policies and decisions, which have far-reaching global implications. This collective bargaining power is especially vital in an era where geopolitical dynamics are increasingly multipolar.

Enhanced Security Cooperation

Rejoining the EU would allow the UK to fully participate in European security and defense mechanisms. This includes access to intelligence-sharing networks and collaborative efforts in counter-terrorism, cyber security, and border management, vital for addressing contemporary security challenges.

Unified Approach to Global Challenges

The EU's collective approach to global challenges like climate change, public health crises, and economic instability aligns with the need for concerted action on such issues. Rejoining the EU would enable the UK to be part of these collaborative efforts, ensuring a stronger and more coordinated response.

Social Benefits

Freedom of Movement

One of the most tangible benefits of EU membership is the freedom of movement. This allows UK citizens to live, work, and study in other EU countries without significant bureaucratic hurdles. Similarly, it would enable citizens from EU countries to contribute to the UK's economy and cultural diversity.

Educational and Cultural Exchange

EU membership provides opportunities for educational and cultural exchange, notably through programs like Erasmus+. These programs enrich the educational experiences of students and foster a sense of European identity and solidarity.

Consumer Benefits

EU membership offers consumer benefits, including a wider range of products, lower prices due to competitive markets, and high consumer protection standards. These aspects contribute to a higher quality of life for UK citizens.

Conclusion

In sum, the potential rejoining of the EU presents various economic, political, and social benefits for the UK. Economically, it promises enhanced trade opportunities, economic stability, and support for key sectors. Politically, it offers renewed influence in international affairs and enhanced security cooperation. Socially, it brings the advantages of freedom of movement, educational opportunities, and consumer benefits. While the feasibility and desirability of such a move are subject to debate, understanding these benefits is crucial in any discussion about the UK's future relationship with the European Union.

Chapter 3:
Legal and Political Mechanisms

Examination of the Procedures and Mechanisms Required for Reversal

The hypothetical reversal of Brexit would entail navigating a complex labyrinth of legal procedures and political mechanisms, both within the United Kingdom and the European Union. This chapter examines these multifaceted processes, offering a insights into what reversing Brexit would legally and politically entail.

Legal Procedures for Reversal

Initiating the Reversal Process

The first step in reversing Brexit would involve a formal decision by the UK government to pursue rejoining the EU. This decision would likely need to be ratified by Parliament, representing a democratic mandate. In the context of the UK's constitutional framework, this could mean passing legislation or a resolution to reverse the previous acts formalizing Brexit.

EU Membership Application

Once the decision is made domestically, the UK would need to apply to rejoin the EU, as per Article 49 of the Treaty on European Union (TEU). This process starts with a formal application to the European Council, clearly stating the intention to rejoin.

Negotiation of Terms

Rejoining the EU is not an automatic process. It would require negotiations on the terms of membership, including financial contributions, adherence to EU laws and policies, and opt-outs or exceptions, if any. These negotiations would be detailed and potentially lengthy, given the complex nature of EU treaties and protocols.

Ratification by EU Institutions and Member States

The terms of rejoining would need to be agreed upon by the existing EU member states and ratified by their national parliaments. Additionally, the European Parliament would also need to give its consent. This process underscores the multilateral nature of the EU and the need for consensus among its members.

Political Mechanisms and Dynamics

Building Domestic Consensus

Politically, the UK government would need to build a consensus for rejoining, both within Parliament and among the public. Given the divisive nature of Brexit, this could be a significant challenge. It might involve public campaigns, consultations, and potentially a referendum to ensure democratic legitimacy.

Diplomatic Engagement with EU Members

Diplomacy would play a crucial role in the reversal process. The UK would need to engage in diplomatic efforts with individual EU member states and EU institutions to garner support for its reapplication. This would involve addressing any concerns or reservations these states might have about the UK rejoining.

Policy Alignment and Compliance

To rejoin the EU, the UK would need to demonstrate compliance with the EU's acquis communautaire – the body of common rights and obligations that bind all EU members. This would involve aligning domestic laws and policies with those of the EU, a process that could require substantial legislative changes.

Addressing Opt-outs and Special Arrangements

The UK's original terms of membership included several opt-outs and special arrangements, such as those related to the euro and the Schengen Area. During the rejoining process, the feasibility and desirability of retaining these opt-outs would be a subject of negotiation, both domestically and with the EU.

Conclusion

In conclusion, the reversal of Brexit would be a complex and unprecedented process, involving a series of legal steps and political maneuvers. Domestically, it would require legislative action, public support, and a clear government mandate. At the EU level, it would involve formal application, negotiation of terms, and ratification by EU institutions and member states. The process would be intricate and time-consuming, reflecting the intricate nature of EU membership and the multifaceted considerations involved in such a significant geopolitical shift.

Challenges and Obstacles in the Process

Reversing Brexit and rejoining the European Union presents a unique set of challenges and obstacles. These range from legal complexities to political hurdles, both within the United Kingdom and across the European Union. Understanding these challenges is crucial to comprehensively assess the feasibility of such a reversal.

Legal Challenges

Negotiating Terms of Re-entry

One of the foremost legal challenges is negotiating the terms of re-entry into the EU. This process is not simply a reversal of the Brexit procedure but requires establishing new terms of membership. These negotiations would likely center around budget contributions, adherence to EU laws, and potential opt-outs, each presenting its own set of complexities.

Alignment with EU Legislation

Since leaving the EU, the UK has begun diverging from EU regulations and standards. Realigning UK laws with the EU's acquis communautaire would be a significant undertaking, requiring extensive legislative amendments. This alignment process could face resistance domestically, particularly in areas where the UK has developed its policies post-Brexit.

EU Member States' Ratification

The agreement for the UK to rejoin the EU would need ratification by all member states, according to their constitutional requirements. This process introduces a multitude of external variables, as each member state may have different perspectives and conditions for the UK's re-entry.

Political Hurdles

Domestic Political Consensus

Achieving a domestic political consensus on rejoining the EU would be a significant challenge. The Brexit referendum and its aftermath have deeply polarized UK politics and society. Any move towards rejoining would require substantial political capital and public support, potentially necessitating another referendum.

Addressing Euroscepticism

Euroscepticism in the UK, a key factor leading to Brexit, remains a potent force. Convincing a skeptical public and political factions of the benefits of rejoining the EU would be a considerable challenge, requiring targeted communication and engagement strategies.

EU's Political Will

There is also the question of political will within the EU. The Brexit process was arduous and strained EU-UK relations. EU member states and institutions may have reservations about the UK rejoining, especially considering the possibility of future volatility and uncertainty.

Economic and Social Obstacles

Economic Policy Adjustments

Economic policy adjustments would be needed to realign the UK with the EU's economic framework. This includes fiscal policies, state aid regulations, and competition law. Such adjustments could face resistance from sectors that have adapted to the post-Brexit regulatory environment.

Social and Cultural Integration

Reintegration into the EU would not only be a political and economic process but also a social and cultural one. The UK would need to navigate the societal implications of rejoining, addressing issues such as freedom of movement and the rights of EU citizens in the UK and vice versa.

Strategic and Diplomatic Considerations

Balancing Global Relationships

The UK has begun establishing new global trade relationships post-Brexit. Rejoining the EU would require balancing these relationships with the obligations and commitments of EU membership, potentially leading to diplomatic challenges.

Long-term EU-UK Dynamics

The long-term dynamics of the EU-UK relationship would be an important consideration. There would be a need to ensure stability and predictability in this relationship, avoiding a repeat of the uncertainty and disruption caused by Brexit.

Conclusion

The process of reversing Brexit and rejoining the EU is fraught with multifaceted challenges and obstacles. Legally, it entails complex negotiations and legislative realignments. Politically, it requires building consensus and navigating euroscepticism both domestically and within the EU. Economically and socially, it involves policy

adjustments and societal integration. Strategically, it requires careful diplomatic balancing and consideration of long-term dynamics.
These challenges underscore the complexity of the issue, reflecting
the intricate nature of national sovereignty, regional integration,
and global interdependence.

Chapter 4: Public Opinion and Political Will

Analysis of Current Public Opinion on Brexit and Its Reversal

Understanding public opinion on Brexit and the prospect of its reversal is crucial for comprehending the political landscape in the United Kingdom. This chapter delves into the nuances of public sentiment, analyzing how opinions have evolved since the 2016 referendum and the factors influencing these changes.

Evolving Public Opinion Since the Referendum

Initial Reactions and Subsequent Shifts

The 2016 referendum, which resulted in a 52% vote for leaving the EU, showcased a nation deeply divided. Initial reactions reflected a mix of surprise, satisfaction, and dismay. However, as the complexities of implementing Brexit unfolded, public opinion showed signs of fluctuation. Factors such as economic impacts, negotiations with the EU, and political developments have influenced these shifts.

Influence of Brexit Outcomes on Public Sentiment

The practical outcomes of Brexit have played a significant role in shaping public opinion. Issues such as trade disruptions, the Northern Ireland protocol, and the loss of free movement have led some to reassess their stance on Brexit. These real-world impacts have provided a concrete basis for the public to evaluate the merits and drawbacks of the decision.

Demographic and Regional Variations

Age, Education, and Regional Differences

Opinions on Brexit and its potential reversal vary significantly across different demographics and regions. Younger voters, who predominantly voted to remain, tend to be more favorable towards the EU and the idea of rejoining. Similarly, there is a notable divide in opinion based on education levels and geographic regions, with Scotland and Northern Ireland, both of which voted to remain, showing higher support for rejoining the EU.

The Brexit Identity and Cultural Factors

Brexit has transcended being a mere political decision, becoming an integral part of personal and cultural identity for many. This 'Brexit identity' has influenced opinions, making the issue a reflection of broader societal values and norms, further complicating the public's stance on reversal.

Impact of Political Leadership and Media

Role of Political Parties and Leaders

Political parties and leaders have significantly influenced public opinion on Brexit. Their stances and rhetoric, both during and after the referendum, have helped shape the narrative around Brexit and its potential reversal. Changes in party leadership and policy positions on Brexit have also impacted public sentiment.

Media Influence and Information Sources

The media has played a pivotal role in forming public opinion on Brexit. Different media outlets, with varying editorial stances, have presented distinct narratives about Brexit and its impacts, influencing how the public perceives and understands the issue.

Public Opinion Polls and Surveys

Trends in Recent Polls

Recent public opinion polls and surveys provide valuable insights into current sentiments towards Brexit and its reversal. These polls indicate a nuanced picture, with some showing a slight shift towards regret or reconsideration, especially among those who initially supported Brexit.

Interpretation of Poll Data

Interpreting poll data requires caution, considering the complexities of public opinion and the potential for shifts over time. Polls are snapshots of sentiment at specific moments and can be influenced by current events, economic conditions, and political developments.

Conclusion

Public opinion on Brexit and the idea of its reversal is dynamic and multifaceted. It is influenced by a range of factors including demographic characteristics, regional identities, political leadership, media narratives, and the tangible outcomes of Brexit. While some polls suggest a shift in sentiment, the issue remains deeply intertwined with national identity and cultural values, reflecting the ongoing complexity and divisiveness of Brexit in the UK's public and political discourse. Understanding these nuances is essential for any meaningful discussion about the future relationship between the UK and the EU, and the potential for reversing Brexit.

The Role of Political Parties and Leaders in Shaping Public Sentiment

The influence of political parties and leaders in shaping public opinion, particularly on issues as significant as Brexit, cannot be understated. This section explores how political figures and party narratives have influenced public sentiment towards Brexit and the idea of its reversal.

The Impact of Party Stances on Brexit

Conservative Party Dynamics

The Conservative Party, traditionally seen as the party of economic stability and free markets, played a pivotal role in the Brexit referendum. Figures like Boris Johnson and Michael Gove, who campaigned vigorously for Leave, significantly influenced public sentiment. Their messaging focused on themes of sovereignty and control, appealing to a sense of national identity. Post-referendum, as the party in government, the Conservatives' approach to Brexit negotiations and their public messaging continued to shape opinions, particularly among their base.

Labour Party's Position

The Labour Party faced its challenges regarding Brexit. Initially under the leadership of Jeremy Corbyn, the party's ambiguous stance on Brexit caused confusion among its voters, many of whom had voted Remain. This ambiguity reflected internal divisions within the party and contributed to a lack of a clear, alternative narrative to that of the Conservatives. Under Keir Starmer, the party has sought to clarify its position, but the impact of its earlier indecisiveness on public sentiment remains significant.

The Influence of Party Leaders

Charismatic Leadership and Persuasion

Charismatic leaders such as Boris Johnson have wielded considerable influence in shaping public opinion on Brexit. Their ability to connect with voters, coupled with strong media presence, has been instrumental in framing the Brexit debate. Similarly, figures like Nigel Farage, despite not being a Member of Parliament, significantly swayed public opinion through his leadership of UKIP and later the Brexit Party.

Opposition Leaders' Role

The role of opposition leaders in shaping Brexit sentiment has been complex. The opposition's critique of the government's handling of Brexit negotiations and the highlighting of potential negative impacts have informed public debate. However, their effectiveness in swaying public sentiment has been mixed, partly due to the polarizing nature of Brexit.

Role of Smaller Parties and Regional Leaders

Scottish National Party (SNP) and Brexit

In Scotland, the SNP has consistently opposed Brexit, using it to bolster the case for Scottish independence. The party's stance and its portrayal of Brexit as contrary to Scotland's will have significantly influenced public opinion in Scotland, leading to increased support for both EU membership and Scottish independence.

Other Regional Parties

In Northern Ireland and Wales, regional parties like Sinn Féin and Plaid Cymru have also shaped public sentiment. Their perspectives on Brexit, influenced by regional considerations and the potential impact on the Good Friday Agreement in Northern Ireland, have contributed to the diverse range of opinions on Brexit across the UK.

Media and Political Messaging

The Role of Media in Amplifying Messages

The media has played a critical role in amplifying the messages of political parties and leaders. The way Brexit has been reported and discussed in the media, including the portrayal of leaders and their stances, has significantly influenced public perception and understanding of the issue.

Social Media and Direct Engagement

Social media has allowed political parties and leaders to engage directly with the public, bypassing traditional media filters. This direct engagement has enabled them to shape public sentiment more effectively, although it has also contributed to the spread of misinformation and the polarization of opinions.

Conclusion

In conclusion, political parties and their leaders have been instrumental in shaping public sentiment towards Brexit and the notion of its reversal. Through their stances, messaging, and engagement with the public and media, they have influenced how Brexit is perceived and understood by the populace. This influence has not only shaped the political landscape in the UK but has also had profound implications for the nature of public discourse and democratic engagement in the context of this significant geopolitical issue. Understanding this dynamic is crucial for comprehending the current and future trajectory of the UK's relationship with the EU.

Chapter 5: Economic Implications

Analysis of the Economic Impact of Brexit

Brexit has had profound and far-reaching economic implications for the United Kingdom, fundamentally altering its trade, investment, and economic policy landscape. This chapter provides an analysis of these economic impacts, offering a broad view of how Brexit has reshaped the UK's economic situation.

Impact on Trade

Trade Barriers and Costs

One of the most immediate effects of Brexit was the introduction of new trade barriers between the UK and the EU. Despite the Trade and Cooperation Agreement allowing for tariff-free trade, non-tariff barriers such as customs checks and regulatory divergences have increased the costs and complexity of doing business. This has particularly affected industries reliant on just-in-time supply chains, like automotive and pharmaceuticals.

Changes in Trade Patterns

Brexit has led to shifts in the UK's trade patterns. The increased difficulty in trading with the EU has prompted some businesses to seek markets elsewhere. While this diversification has potential benefits, it does not fully compensate for the loss of frictionless access to the large EU market.

Investment Flows

Decline in Foreign Direct Investment (FDI)

The uncertainty surrounding Brexit negotiations and the post-Brexit economic landscape led to a decline in FDI. Investors have been cautious due to concerns about market access and the UK's future economic policies. This decline in investment has implications for economic growth, job creation, and innovation.

Impact on Financial Services

London's status as a leading global financial center has been challenged by Brexit. The loss of passporting rights, which allowed seamless financial services across the EU, has led some businesses to relocate parts of their operations to EU cities. This relocation affects the UK's tax revenues and employment in the financial sector.

Economic Growth and GDP

Short and Long-term Growth Prospects

Brexit has impacted the UK's economic growth prospects. In the short term, the uncertainty and adjustment to new trading relationships have led to slower growth. The long-term impact on GDP will depend on factors like trade deals, regulatory changes, and productivity growth. Some economic models suggest a long-term reduction in potential GDP due to reduced trade and investment.

Sectoral Impacts

Different sectors of the UK economy have been affected in varying degrees. Industries that rely heavily on exports to the EU, such as agriculture and manufacturing, have faced significant challenges. In contrast, some domestic-focused sectors have been less directly impacted.

Fiscal Implications

Government Revenues and Expenditures

Brexit has implications for public finances. Reduced economic activity can lead to lower tax revenues, while increased costs of doing business can impact government expenditures. Additionally, the UK must now fund initiatives and subsidies previously covered by EU funds, such as in agriculture and regional development.

Currency Fluctuations

The pound sterling has experienced volatility since the Brexit referendum, impacting trade, inflation, and foreign investment. A weaker pound makes imports more expensive, contributing to inflationary pressures, but can benefit exporters by making their goods cheaper on international markets.

Labour Market Effects

Workforce and Employment

The end of free movement between the UK and the EU has had a significant impact on the labor market. Industries like agriculture, healthcare, and hospitality, which relied heavily on EU workers, have faced staff shortages. This has led to calls for changes in immigration policy to address these gaps.

Wage and Productivity Implications

There is ongoing debate about the impact of Brexit on wages and productivity. Some argue that reduced immigration could lead to higher wages for domestic workers, while others suggest that reduced labor supply and lower economic growth could have the opposite effect.

Regional Implications

Variations Across the UK

The impact of Brexit is not uniform across the UK. Regions with strong ties to EU markets, such as the manufacturing hubs in the Midlands and the North of England, are particularly vulnerable. In contrast, some sectors concentrated in London, like finance and tech, may be more resilient.

Conclusion

Brexit has had significant and multifaceted economic impacts on the United Kingdom. From trade and investment to fiscal policy and the labor market, the effects are widespread and complex. While some sectors and regions are more affected than others, the overall economic landscape of the UK has been indelibly altered. Understanding these impacts is crucial for policymakers, businesses, and citizens as the UK navigates its post-Brexit future.

Potential Economic Benefits and Challenges of Rejoining the EU

The hypothetical scenario of the United Kingdom rejoining the European Union opens a discussion about potential economic benefits and challenges. This chapter aims to dissect these possibilities, offering a balanced perspective on what reintegration could mean for the UK's economy.

Potential Economic Benefits

Restoration of Trade Benefits

Rejoining the EU would mean re-entering the Single Market and Customs Union, thereby eliminating many of the trade barriers that arose post-Brexit. This change could reduce costs and complexities for businesses, enhance supply chain efficiency, and potentially increase trade volumes with EU member states.

Increase in Foreign Direct Investment (FDI)

The certainty and stability associated with EU membership could lead to an increase in FDI. Investors generally favor stable and predictable markets, and the UK's re-entry into the EU could signal a return to such conditions, potentially rejuvenating investment in various sectors.

Financial Services Sector

Reintegrating into the EU could revive London's position as a leading global financial hub. Regaining passporting rights would allow financial firms in the UK unrestricted access to EU markets, bolstering the sector's growth and contribution to the economy.

Agricultural and Research Funding

EU membership comes with access to various funding streams, including the Common Agricultural Policy (CAP) and research and development funds. Rejoining could provide UK farmers and researchers access to these funds, supporting these critical sectors.

Labor Market Benefits

Freedom of movement within the EU could address some of the labor shortages experienced in the UK post-Brexit. Industries like healthcare, agriculture, and hospitality, which previously relied heavily on EU workers, could benefit significantly from this change.

Challenges of Rejoining

Negotiation of Membership Terms

Rejoining the EU would not be a simple reversal of Brexit. It would involve renegotiating the terms of membership, which could be a complex and time-consuming process. Issues like budget contributions, adherence to EU regulations, and acceptance of the four freedoms would be key negotiation points.

Economic Adjustment Period

Reintegrating into the EU economy would require an adjustment period. Businesses that have adapted to the post-Brexit environment may need to recalibrate their operations again. This transition could lead to temporary disruptions and adjustment costs.

Political and Public Resistance

There could be significant political and public resistance to rejoining the EU, especially given the divisive nature of Brexit. Overcoming this resistance would be a major challenge, necessitating extensive public engagement and potentially another referendum.

Loss of New Trade Agreements

Post-Brexit, the UK has begun forging new trade agreements outside the EU framework. Rejoining the EU would mean relinquishing the independent trade policy and potentially losing the benefits of these new agreements.

Financial Contributions and Economic Policy Sovereignty

EU membership requires financial contributions to the EU budget, which could be a contentious issue given the current economic climate. Additionally, rejoining would mean ceding some level of economic policy sovereignty back to the EU, a move that may face criticism from those who value national regulatory autonomy.

Weighing the Benefits and Challenges

Economic Integration vs. Sovereignty

The decision to rejoin the EU involves balancing the benefits of economic integration with the desire for national sovereignty in economic policymaking. This balance is a central theme in the debate over the potential economic impacts of rejoining.

Long-term Economic Prospects

The long-term economic implications of rejoining the EU are subject to debate. Proponents argue that the benefits of market access and stability outweigh the costs, while critics emphasize the importance of independent economic policy and global trade opportunities.

Conclusion

The potential rejoining of the EU by the UK presents a complex array of economic benefits and challenges. While reintegration could bring trade benefits, increased investment, and labor market advantages, it also poses significant challenges in terms of negotiations, economic adjustments, and political feasibility. The decision would require a careful weighing of the prospects for economic stability and growth against the implications for economic policy sovereignty and the UK's global trade ambitions. Understanding these economic dynamics is crucial for any discourse on the UK's potential reintegration into the European Union.

Chapter 6:
Diplomatic Dynamics

EU's Perspective on the UK Potentially Rejoining

The European Union's perspective on the United Kingdom potentially rejoining is a critical aspect of the broader discussion about reversing Brexit. This chapter explores the EU's viewpoint, considering various political, economic, and institutional factors that would influence its stance on the UK's potential return.

Political Considerations in the EU

EU's Stance on Member State Sovereignty

The EU fundamentally respects the sovereignty of its member states and their decisions regarding EU membership. This principle would guide the EU's response to any UK overtures about rejoining. The EU's primary concern would be ensuring that the decision is a result of a clear and democratic process within the UK.

Precedent and Stability Concerns

The UK rejoining would set a significant precedent within the EU. EU institutions would be concerned about the implications for the stability and cohesion of the union, especially considering the lengthy and complex process of Brexit.

Internal Political Dynamics

The EU's internal political dynamics would play a vital role in shaping its perspective. Member states' governments may have varying views on the UK's potential return, influenced by their national interests, public opinion, and historical relationships with the UK.

Economic Implications for the EU

Impact on the Single Market

The UK's re-entry into the Single Market would have considerable economic implications for the EU. While the return of a major economy would be beneficial, it would also require adjustments, particularly in sectors where the post-Brexit period led to realignments.

Budgetary Considerations

The UK was one of the largest net contributors to the EU budget. Its potential return would have significant budgetary implications, both in terms of contributions and the distribution of funding across EU policies and programs.

Trade and Investment

The UK's rejoining would impact EU trade and investment dynamics. The EU would consider how the UK's return could enhance the union's global trade position and the potential benefits of increased investment flows.

Institutional and Legal Aspects

Adherence to EU Regulations and Standards

The EU would require the UK to fully adhere to its regulations and standards as part of the rejoining process. This would include alignment with EU laws, policies, and values, which could be a complex process given the UK's regulatory divergences post-Brexit.

Negotiation of Rejoining Terms

The terms of the UK's rejoining would need to be negotiated, a process likely to be as intricate as the Brexit negotiations. These negotiations would cover a wide range of issues, from financial contributions to participation in EU institutions and agencies.

The EU's Strategic Interests

Strengthening the European Project

The EU's response to the UK potentially rejoining would be influenced by its strategic interest in strengthening the European project. The return of the UK could be seen as a reaffirmation of the EU's attractiveness and resilience.

Global Geopolitical Considerations

In a changing global geopolitical landscape, the EU would consider how the UK's rejoining aligns with its broader strategic interests. This includes the EU's role on the international stage, its relationships with major powers, and its global economic positioning.

Challenges and Concerns

Trust and Reliability Issues

The Brexit process strained the EU-UK relationship, and there may be concerns within the EU about the UK's reliability as a member state. Trust would be a crucial factor in any discussions about rejoining.

Addressing Euroscepticism

The EU would also be wary of the impact of UK rejoining on eurosceptic sentiments within other member states. It would be essential to manage this process in a way that reinforces, rather than undermines, EU cohesion and unity.

Conclusion

The European Union's perspective on the UK potentially rejoining is shaped by a complex interplay of political, economic, institutional, and strategic considerations. While the return of the UK would bring certain benefits, it would also pose challenges and raise concerns about precedent, stability, and trust. The EU's response would be guided by its fundamental principles, the interests of its member states, and its overarching strategic goals. Understanding this perspective is crucial for any analysis of the potential for the UK to reverse Brexit and reintegrate into the European Union.

International Diplomatic Considerations and Implications

The prospect of the United Kingdom rejoining the European Union carries with it significant international diplomatic considerations and implications. This complex web of geopolitical dynamics shapes and is shaped by global relationships and strategic interests. This section explores these international dimensions and their potential impact on the global stage.

Global Geopolitical Landscape

Shifting Power Dynamics

The UK's potential re-entry into the EU would occur against a backdrop of shifting global power dynamics. In an increasingly multipolar world, the combined economic and political weight of the EU, with the UK as a member, could alter balances of power, especially in relation to the United States, China, and Russia.

Influence on Global Institutions

The UK's role in global institutions like the United Nations, NATO, and the World Trade Organization could be influenced by its relationship with the EU. As a member of the EU, the UK might align more closely with EU positions, potentially affecting its stance on various international issues.

Trade Agreements and Economic Partnerships

Impact on Existing Agreements

The UK's rejoining the EU would have implications for the trade agreements it negotiated post-Brexit. Realigning with the EU's common commercial policy would require revisiting these agreements, which could lead to complex renegotiations with global partners.

Future Trade Strategies

The UK's trade strategy would need to align with that of the EU, impacting its approach to future trade deals. This could lead to shifts in priorities and tactics, affecting global trade patterns and partnerships.

Diplomatic Relations and Alliances

Transatlantic Relations

The UK's relationship with the United States is a key aspect of its foreign policy. Rejoining the EU could alter this dynamic, particularly in areas where US and EU policies diverge, such as trade and regulatory standards.

Commonwealth Countries

The UK's ties with Commonwealth countries, which received renewed focus post-Brexit, could be affected by rejoining the EU. Balancing these historical ties with commitments to the EU would be a diplomatic challenge.

Regional Alliances and Partnerships

Reintegration into the EU would also affect the UK's role in regional alliances and partnerships. Its approach to issues in the Middle East, Africa, and Asia would likely be more coordinated with EU positions.

Security and Defense Considerations

NATO and European Defense

While NATO remains the cornerstone of European defense, the UK's rejoining the EU could influence its participation in EU defense initiatives. This would have implications for European security architecture and the UK's defense relationships.

Counter-Terrorism and Cybersecurity

Collaboration in counter-terrorism and cybersecurity could be enhanced by the UK's reintegration. Sharing intelligence and resources within EU frameworks would bolster collective security efforts.

Environmental and Global Health Diplomacy

Climate Change and Environmental Policies

The UK's approach to global environmental challenges, particularly climate change, would be aligned more closely with EU policies. This could strengthen global environmental initiatives and agreements.

Pandemic Response and Public Health

In the realm of public health, particularly in response to pandemics, the UK's rejoining the EU could lead to more coordinated strategies and policies, impacting global health diplomacy.

Challenges and Opportunities

Navigating Sovereignty and Supranationalism

The UK would need to navigate the balance between national sovereignty and supranational EU commitments in its foreign policy, a task that presents both challenges and opportunities for diplomatic maneuvering.

Influence in EU Foreign Policy

As a member of the EU, the UK would have the opportunity to shape EU foreign policy from within. This could enhance its influence on international issues, aligning with its global ambitions.

Conclusion

The potential rejoining of the UK to the EU holds far-reaching international diplomatic considerations and implications. It would affect global geopolitical dynamics, trade relationships, diplomatic alliances, security arrangements, and environmental and public health strategies. The interplay of these factors would shape not only the UK's foreign policy but also the broader global order. Understanding these diplomatic dynamics is essential for comprehending the full spectrum of implications associated with the UK's potential reintegration into the European Union.

Chapter 7:
Case Studies and Comparisons

Examination of Other Countries' Experiences with Major Political and Economic Reversals

The contemplation of the United Kingdom potentially reversing Brexit and rejoining the European Union invites a broader examination of similar major political and economic reversals in other countries. Such case studies offer valuable insights into the challenges, strategies, and outcomes of these significant shifts. This chapter explores a selection of these international experiences, drawing comparisons and lessons that could be relevant to the UK's situation.

Greece's Austerity Referendum, 2015

Background and Decision

In 2015, Greece held a referendum on whether to accept bailout conditions set by its creditors, primarily the EU and the IMF. The Greek public voted overwhelmingly against the austerity measures. However, the Greek government, facing economic collapse and potential exit from the Eurozone ('Grexit'), eventually agreed to a modified version of the bailout conditions.

Lessons Learned

This case illustrates the complex interplay between democratic mandates, economic realities, and international negotiations. It underscores the challenges countries face when balancing national sovereignty with the demands of international economic systems.

Canada's Quebec Referendums, 1980 and 1995

Background and Decision

Quebec held referendums in 1980 and 1995 to decide on seceding from Canada. Both times, the secessionist movement was narrowly defeated. The referendums led to significant political negotiations, resulting in constitutional amendments and changes to the federal relationship between Quebec and the Canadian government.

Lessons Learned

These referendums demonstrate the enduring impact of regional separatist movements within a country. They also show how referendums can lead to political and constitutional reforms, even when the status quo is maintained.

Norway's EU Membership Referendums, 1972 and 1994

Background and Decision

Norway held referendums on joining the EU in 1972 and 1994. In both instances, the public voted against membership. Despite this, Norway maintained close ties with the EU through the European Economic Area (EEA) agreement.

Lessons Learned

Norway's experience highlights how countries can maintain close economic relationships with larger unions without full membership. It also illustrates the importance of finding alternative models of cooperation that align with national interests and public sentiment.

India's Economic Liberalization, 1991

Background and Decision

In 1991, facing a severe economic crisis, India shifted from a closed, socialist economy to a market-driven one. This major reversal involved liberalizing trade, devaluing the currency, and encouraging foreign investments.

Lessons Learned

India's case is an example of how economic crises can precipitate significant policy reversals. It shows the potential for economic liberalization to spur growth and modernization, albeit with challenges such as rising inequality and environmental concerns.

South Africa's End of Apartheid, 1994

Background and Decision

The end of apartheid in South Africa in 1994 was a major political and economic reversal. It involved dismantling racial segregation, introducing democracy, and reforming economic policies to be more inclusive.

Lessons Learned

South Africa's transition highlights the challenges of transforming a deeply divided society and economy. It underscores the importance of inclusive governance and the need for economic policies that address historical inequalities.

Argentina's Economic Policies Reversal, Early 2000s

Background and Decision

In the early 2000s, Argentina experienced a major economic crisis, leading to a reversal of its neoliberal policies. The government defaulted on its debt, devalued the currency, and implemented protectionist policies.

Lessons Learned

Argentina's experience shows how economic crises can lead to dramatic policy reversals. It also illustrates the challenges of balancing external debt obligations with domestic economic needs and the potential for populist policies in times of economic hardship.

Conclusion

These case studies from around the world provide valuable lessons on navigating major political and economic reversals. They demonstrate the complexities and nuances involved in such processes, including the interplay of domestic politics, economic realities, and international relations. For the UK, contemplating the potential reversal of Brexit and rejoining the EU, these examples offer insights into the challenges and strategies that could be employed, as well as the diverse outcomes that might ensue. Understanding these global experiences is crucial for policymakers and stakeholders in shaping a well-informed approach to any significant geopolitical shift.

Lessons Learned and Applicable Strategies

In the context of major political and economic reversals, like the hypothetical scenario of the UK rejoining the EU post-Brexit, there are valuable lessons to be learned from international experiences. This section synthesizes these lessons and explores applicable strategies that could guide such a significant geopolitical shift.

Understanding the Interplay of Domestic and International Factors

Integrating National and Global Interests

Case studies like Greece's austerity referendum and Norway's EU membership referendums highlight the need to balance national sovereignty with international economic and political realities. An effective strategy involves aligning domestic policies with global economic systems and diplomatic relations, ensuring that national interests are harmoniously integrated with international commitments.

Embracing Flexibility and Adaptability

Navigating Changing Circumstances

The situations in Canada with Quebec and in South Africa post-apartheid demonstrate the importance of flexibility in political decision-making. Adapting to changing circumstances and public sentiment is crucial. For the UK, this means being open to evolving economic and political landscapes and adjusting strategies accordingly.

Prioritizing Inclusive and Transparent Processes

Engaging Diverse Stakeholders

Inclusive governance, as seen in South Africa's transition, is key to ensuring broad support and legitimacy. The UK's strategy for rejoining the EU should involve transparent negotiations and active engagement with various stakeholders, including political factions, businesses, and the public, to build a consensus.

Economic Policy Reforms and Crisis Management

Learning from Economic Transitions

India's economic liberalization and Argentina's policy reversals during their economic crisis offer insights into managing economic policy shifts. The UK should focus on reforms that stimulate growth and modernization while being mindful of social implications like inequality. Crisis management should balance immediate economic needs with long-term sustainability.

Leveraging Alternative Models of Cooperation

Exploring Varied Forms of Engagement

Norway's relationship with the EU through the EEA agreement shows that there are alternative models for cooperation beyond full membership. The UK could explore varied forms of engagement with the EU, potentially providing a template for a new kind of relationship that offers mutual benefits without full integration.

Addressing Socio-Political Divisions

Fostering National Cohesion

Canada's approach to the Quebec referendums underlines the importance of addressing regional and national divisions. The UK's strategy should include policies and narratives that foster national cohesion and address the concerns of different regions and demographic groups.

Economic Diversification and Global Trade

Balancing Trade Relationships

The experiences of countries like India and Argentina emphasize the importance of economic diversification and the pursuit of balanced global trade relationships. For the UK, this means continuing to develop trade ties outside the EU while also seeking to rebuild and enhance its relationship with the EU.

Strategic Communication and Public Engagement

Managing Public Perception

Effective communication and public engagement are vital, as seen in most case studies. The UK government should employ strategic communication to manage public perception, providing clear, accurate information about the implications and benefits of rejoining the EU.

Leveraging Diplomatic Relations

Strengthening International Alliances

The role of international alliances and diplomatic relations is evident in scenarios like South Africa's transition and Argentina's economic crisis. The UK should leverage its diplomatic relations to garner support and understanding for its decision to rejoin the EU, both within Europe and globally.

Building Institutional Resilience

Preparing for Long-term Impacts

Institutional resilience is crucial for managing the long-term impacts of major policy reversals, as shown in all the case studies. The UK should focus on strengthening its political and economic institutions to ensure they can withstand and adapt to the changes and challenges of rejoining the EU.

Conclusion

In conclusion, the analysis of international experiences with major political and economic reversals provides a wealth of lessons and applicable strategies. For the UK, considering a potential reversal of Brexit and rejoining the EU, these lessons emphasize the importance of balancing domestic and international factors, embracing flexibility, ensuring inclusive processes, managing economic transitions, exploring alternative cooperation models, addressing socio-political divisions, diversifying the economy, engaging in strategic communication, leveraging diplomatic relations, and building institutional resilience. These strategies can guide the UK in navigating the complexities and challenges of such a significant geopolitical shift.

Chapter 8:
The Roadmap to Rejoining

Step-by-Step Analysis of the Potential Process to Reverse Brexit

Reversing Brexit and rejoining the European Union would be an unprecedented and complex process. This section outlines a step-by-step analysis of how such a scenario might unfold, detailing the procedural and diplomatic steps involved.

Step 1: Domestic Decision-Making

Assessing the Public and Political Will

The first step involves assessing the public and political will for rejoining the EU. This could be initiated through public opinion polls, consultations, and potentially a new referendum. The government would need to ensure there is a clear mandate for rejoining.

Parliamentary Approval

Should there be a demonstrable shift in public and political sentiment, the next step would be for Parliament to debate and vote on the decision to apply for EU membership. This would likely involve drafting and passing legislation or a motion to reverse the Brexit decision.

Step 2: Formal Application to Rejoin the EU

Submitting an Application

Once the domestic consensus is achieved, the UK would formally apply to rejoin the EU under Article 49 of the Treaty on European

Union. This application is submitted to the European Council and marks the official start of the rejoining process.

Step 3: Negotiation of Terms

Setting the Framework for Negotiations

The European Council would then set a framework for negotiations, laying out the terms and conditions for the UK's re-entry. These negotiations would be comprehensive, covering everything from financial contributions to adherence to EU policies and standards.

The Role of the European Commission

The European Commission would likely lead the negotiations on behalf of the EU, working out the details of the UK's rejoining agreement. These negotiations would be intricate and could take a considerable amount of time to complete.

Step 4: Ratification by EU Institutions

European Parliament Approval

Once a rejoining agreement is reached, it would need the approval of the European Parliament. The Parliament would scrutinize the agreement to ensure it aligns with EU interests and policies.

European Council Approval

The agreement would also require the approval of the European Council, which consists of the heads of state or government of all EU member states. Their unanimous approval is necessary for the rejoining process to proceed.

Step 5: Ratification by EU Member States

National Parliaments' Ratification

Each EU member state must ratify the agreement according to its national procedures, which could involve votes in national parliaments. This step underscores the importance of securing broad support among all EU members.

Step 6: Domestic Legal Adjustments

Aligning UK Laws with EU Standards

Parallel to the negotiations, the UK would need to begin the process of realigning its laws and regulations with the EU's acquis communautaire. This would likely involve substantial legislative changes across various sectors.

Step 7: Institutional Integration

Rejoining EU Institutions and Agencies

The UK would need to reintegrate into EU institutions and agencies. This includes regaining representation in the European Parliament, European Commission, and other bodies, as well as participating in various EU programs and initiatives.

Step 8: Addressing Transitional Challenges

Managing Economic and Social Impacts

Throughout the process, the UK government would need to manage the economic and social impacts of transitioning back to EU membership. This includes addressing any disruptions to trade, business operations, and the labor market.

Step 9: Finalization and Implementation

Finalizing the Rejoining Process

Once all ratifications are in place and legal adjustments are made, the process would be finalized with the UK officially becoming an EU member state again. This final step would be marked by a formal announcement and likely a significant political ceremony.

Implementation of the Agreement

The final step involves the implementation of the rejoining agreement, ensuring that all aspects of the agreement are put into practice. This includes the practical aspects of EU membership, such as participation in the customs union and single market, adherence to EU policies, and contribution to the EU budget.

Conclusion

In conclusion, reversing Brexit and rejoining the EU would be a multifaceted and time-consuming process, involving a series of procedural, legal, and diplomatic steps. It would require a clear domestic mandate, comprehensive negotiations, widespread ratification, and careful management of transitional challenges. This roadmap outlines the potential steps involved, highlighting the complexity and magnitude of such a geopolitical shift.

Short-term and Long-term Strategies

In considering the reversal of Brexit and the UK's rejoining of the European Union, it is imperative to delineate both short-term and long-term strategies. These strategies should address the immediate logistical challenges and lay the foundation for sustainable integration into the EU. This chapter outlines these strategies, offering a roadmap for navigating this complex transition.

Short-Term Strategies

Establishing a Clear Mandate

Immediate Public Engagement: Engaging with the public to gauge the current sentiment towards rejoining the EU is crucial. This may involve conducting opinion polls, organizing public forums, and potentially a new referendum to ensure a democratic mandate.

Parliamentary Consensus: Securing broad parliamentary support is essential. This involves not only the ruling party but also opposition parties, to create a unified national approach towards the rejoining process.

Formal Application Process

Preparing the Application: The UK government must prepare a comprehensive application to rejoin the EU, detailing its commitment to EU standards and regulations.

Diplomatic Outreach: Initiating diplomatic discussions with EU member states and institutions is critical to garner support for the rejoining process.

Negotiation Preparation

Formation of Negotiation Team: A skilled negotiation team should be formed, including experts in EU law, trade, economics, and diplomacy.

Setting Negotiation Goals: Clearly defined goals for the rejoining negotiations need to be established, covering key areas such as trade, immigration, and financial contributions.

Long-Term Strategies

Legal and Regulatory Alignment

Review and Alignment of Laws: A thorough review of UK laws and regulations is needed to identify areas requiring alignment with EU legislation.

Legislative Process: Implementing necessary changes in domestic laws and regulations to ensure compliance with EU standards.

Economic and Fiscal Planning

Economic Impact Assessment: Conducting comprehensive assessments to understand the economic impacts of rejoining, both positive and negative.

Fiscal Adjustments: Preparing for the financial implications of EU membership, including budget contributions and adjustments to accommodate EU funding mechanisms.

Institutional Integration

Rebuilding Institutional Relationships: Reestablishing the UK's presence in EU institutions and working groups.

Training and Capacity Building: Ensuring UK representatives and officials are adequately trained and prepared for participation in EU institutions.

Social and Cultural Integration

Public Communication Campaigns: Developing communication strategies to inform and educate the public about the implications and benefits of rejoining the EU.

Cultural and Educational Exchange Programs: Promoting cultural and educational exchanges with EU member states to foster a sense of shared European identity.

Trade and Diplomatic Relations

Trade Strategy Revision: Revising the UK's global trade strategy to align with EU policies and priorities.

Diplomatic Efforts: Strengthening diplomatic ties with EU member states and other global partners to support the UK's reintegration into the EU.

Addressing Regional Disparities

Regional Engagement: Addressing concerns and interests of different UK regions, particularly Scotland and Northern Ireland, in the rejoining process.

Economic Development Programs: Developing programs to support regions and sectors most impacted by the transition back to EU membership.

Monitoring and Evaluation

Ongoing Assessment: Regularly assessing the progress and impact of the rejoining process, adjusting strategies as necessary.

Feedback Mechanisms: Establishing channels for feedback from businesses, civil society, and the public to inform ongoing policy decisions.

Conclusion

In conclusion, a comprehensive approach encompassing both short-term and long-term strategies is essential for the UK's potential reversal of Brexit and rejoining of the EU. These strategies should address the immediate logistical and diplomatic challenges, ensure legal and regulatory alignment, prepare for economic and fiscal impacts, foster institutional and social integration, and maintain robust trade and diplomatic relations. Additionally, continuous monitoring and adaptation to emerging challenges and opportunities will be crucial in navigating this complex and historic transition.

Chapter 9: Challenges and Counterarguments

Addressing the Major Challenges and Counterarguments Against Reversing Brexit

The debate surrounding the potential reversal of Brexit is fraught with significant challenges and counterarguments. Addressing these concerns is crucial for a comprehensive understanding of the implications of such a decision. This section delves into the primary challenges and counterarguments against reversing Brexit, offering insights and responses to these critical points.

Challenge 1: Sovereignty and Democratic Mandate

Counterargument: Undermining the 2016 Referendum

A key argument against reversing Brexit is that it would undermine the democratic mandate of the 2016 referendum, where a majority voted to leave the EU.

Response:

- **Democratic Evolution:** Democracy is not static, and public opinion can evolve. A new referendum or a general election could provide an updated mandate.

- **Informed Decision-Making:** The 2016 referendum was based on certain expectations and predictions. With new information and experience post-Brexit, the public is in a better position to make an informed decision.

Challenge 2: Economic Uncertainty and Disruption

Counterargument: Economic Risks of Reversing Course

Critics argue that reversing Brexit could create economic uncertainty and disrupt the new trade relationships established post-Brexit.

Response:

- **Long-term Economic Stability:** While there may be short-term disruptions, rejoining the EU could offer long-term economic stability and benefits through access to the Single Market and Customs Union.
- **Gradual Transition:** A carefully managed and gradual transition back to EU membership could minimize economic disruptions.

Challenge 3: Political and Social Polarization

Counterargument: Deepening Divisions

Another concern is that attempting to reverse Brexit could further polarize an already divided society and political landscape.

Response:

- **Inclusive Dialogue:** Engaging in a broad and inclusive dialogue that addresses the concerns and aspirations of all societal groups can help mitigate polarization.
- **Addressing Underlying Issues:** Tackling the underlying issues that contributed to the Brexit vote, such as regional inequality and feelings of disenfranchisement, is essential regardless of EU membership status.

Challenge 4: Loss of Global Trade Opportunities

Counterargument: Limiting Global Reach

Some argue that reversing Brexit would limit the UK's ability to establish its own global trade agreements.

> **Response:**

- **Leveraging EU's Global Influence:** As part of the EU, the UK can leverage the bloc's significant global trade influence to benefit from comprehensive trade agreements.
- **Balancing Trade Interests:** The UK can balance its global trade ambitions with the benefits of being part of the EU's trade framework.

Challenge 5: Legal and Bureaucratic Complexities

Counterargument: Legal Entanglements

Reversing Brexit would involve complex legal processes to realign UK laws with EU regulations, seen by some as a bureaucratic nightmare.

> **Response:**

- **Systematic Legal Alignment:** A systematic and phased approach to legal alignment can mitigate complexities.
- **Expertise and Experience:** Leveraging legal and bureaucratic expertise, including learnings from the initial Brexit process, can streamline the alignment process.

Challenge 6: EU's Readiness to Accept the UK Back

Counterargument: EU Reluctance

There is a concern that the EU may be reluctant to accept the UK back, given the tumultuous Brexit process.

- **Diplomatic Engagement:** Through proactive diplomatic engagement, the UK can address the concerns of EU member states and institutions.
- **Demonstrating Commitment:** Showing a clear commitment to EU values and policies can help rebuild trust and facilitate the rejoining process.

Challenge 7: Impact on Domestic Policies

Counterargument: Disruption to National Policies

Rejoining the EU would mean conforming to EU policies and regulations, potentially disrupting national policies developed post-Brexit.

Response:

- **Policy Harmonization:** Harmonizing national policies with EU standards can bring benefits in terms of regulatory consistency and quality standards.
- **Influence in Policy Formation:** As an EU member, the UK would have a say in the formation of policies, allowing it to shape EU regulations in line with its interests.

Conclusion

While there are significant challenges and counterarguments against reversing Brexit, each can be addressed through careful consideration, inclusive dialogue, and strategic planning. Balancing national sovereignty with the benefits of EU membership, managing economic transitions, addressing societal divisions, leveraging global trade opportunities, navigating legal complexities, rebuilding trust with the EU, and harmonizing domestic policies are all achievable with a clear and concerted approach. Understanding and addressing these challenges is crucial for any discourse on the potential reversal of Brexit.

Strategies to Overcome These Challenges

Confronting the challenges associated with potentially reversing Brexit requires a nuanced, multi-faceted approach. This section outlines strategic approaches to overcome the hurdles identified in the previous sections, ensuring a balanced and effective path forward should the UK pursue rejoining the European Union.

Strategy 1: Comprehensive Public Engagement and Communication

Building a New Democratic Mandate

To address concerns about undermining the 2016 referendum, it's crucial to establish a new, informed democratic mandate. This can be achieved through:

- **Nationwide Dialogues:** Conducting open dialogues across the UK to discuss the implications of reversing Brexit.
- **Educational Campaigns:** Implementing educational campaigns to provide unbiased information about the benefits and challenges of rejoining the EU.
- **Referendum or General Election:** Organizing a new referendum or using a general election to secure a clear, democratic mandate for rejoining.

Strategy 2: Economic Impact Assessment and Transitional Planning

Minimizing Economic Disruption

To counter economic uncertainties and disruptions, a detailed economic impact assessment and robust transitional planning are necessary:

- **Impact Studies:** Conducting comprehensive studies to understand the short-term and long-term economic impacts of rejoining.

- **Transitional Economic Policies:** Developing policies to support sectors and regions most likely to be affected during the transition period.

- **Stakeholder Collaboration:** Collaborating with businesses, trade unions, and economic experts to develop strategies that minimize disruption.

Strategy 3: Addressing Political and Social Polarization

Fostering National Unity

To mitigate political and social polarization:

- **Inclusive Political Process:** Ensuring all political parties and social groups are involved in the decision-making process.

- **Regional Consultations:** Engaging with different regions, especially those with strong Leave or Remain sentiments, to address specific concerns.

- **Social Cohesion Programs:** Implementing programs aimed at bridging societal divides and promoting national unity.

Strategy 4: Balancing Global and European Trade Interests

Maximizing Trade Opportunities

To address concerns about global trade opportunities:

- **Dual Trade Strategy:** Developing a strategy that balances the benefits of the EU's trade agreements with pursuing independent trade relationships where beneficial.

- **Leveraging EU Trade Agreements:** Utilizing the EU's extensive network of trade agreements for the UK's economic advantage.

Strategy 5: Streamlining Legal and Bureaucratic Processes

Simplifying Legal Alignment

To manage the complexities of realigning with EU laws:

- **Phased Legal Integration:** Adopting a phased approach to align UK laws with EU standards.
- **Expert Committees:** Forming committees with legal experts to oversee and streamline the alignment process.
- **Public Consultation on Legal Changes:** Engaging the public and stakeholders in the legal change process to ensure transparency and acceptance.

Strategy 6: Building Trust with the EU

Re-establishing a Positive Relationship

To rebuild trust with the EU:

- **Proactive Diplomacy:** Engaging in proactive and positive diplomacy with EU member states and institutions.
- **Commitment to EU Values:** Demonstrating a clear commitment to EU values and policies in the rejoining process.
- **Constructive Participation:** Showing willingness to contribute constructively to the EU's future development.

Strategy 7: Harmonizing National and EU Policies

Aligning Domestic Policies with EU Standards

To address the impact on domestic policies:

- **Policy Review and Alignment:** Reviewing national policies to identify areas for alignment with EU standards.
- **Stakeholder Engagement:** Involving various stakeholders in the policy harmonization process to ensure smooth implementation.

- **Flexibility in Policy Adaptation:** Maintaining flexibility to adapt policies in a way that respects both national interests and EU requirements.

Strategy 8: Strategic Monitoring and Evaluation

Assessing Progress and Making Adjustments

To ensure the effectiveness of these strategies:

- **Regular Monitoring:** Establishing mechanisms for regular monitoring of the rejoining process.
- **Feedback Loops:** Creating feedback loops to gather input from various sectors and make necessary adjustments.
- **Independent Evaluations:** Conducting independent evaluations to assess the impacts of the strategies and make evidence-based decisions.

Conclusion

In conclusion, overcoming the challenges of reversing Brexit and rejoining the EU requires a comprehensive set of strategies that address democratic legitimacy, economic stability, social cohesion, global trade, legal and bureaucratic complexities, diplomatic relations, and policy alignment. These strategies should be grounded in robust public engagement, careful planning, inclusive dialogue, and flexible policymaking. By adopting these approaches, the UK can navigate the complexities of this significant geopolitical shift in a way that maximizes benefits and minimizes disruptions.

Chapter 10: The Future of the UK and EU

Speculation on the Long-Term Relationship

The future relationship between the United Kingdom and the European Union, especially in the context of a potential Brexit reversal, is a subject of considerable speculation. This section explores various scenarios and their potential implications, offering insights into the long-term dynamics of this pivotal relationship.

Scenario 1: Full Reintegration into the EU

Enhanced Cooperation and Influence

If the UK fully reintegrates into the EU, it could regain significant influence within the union. As one of the largest economies in Europe, the UK's participation in decision-making processes would be crucial. This scenario could see the UK actively shaping EU policies, particularly in areas like trade, environmental regulation, and security.

Economic and Social Benefits

Full reintegration would likely bring substantial economic benefits to both the UK and the EU. The UK would regain full access to the Single Market, potentially boosting trade and investment. Socially, the resumption of free movement could enrich cultural exchanges and educational opportunities.

Scenario 2: Partial Association with the EU

A Tailored Relationship

A more likely scenario could be a partial association, where the UK aligns with the EU in specific sectors such as trade, research, and security, without full membership. This relationship could resemble the models of Norway or Switzerland, balancing access to certain benefits of the EU with a degree of independence.

Challenges in Balancing Interests

This scenario would require careful negotiation to balance the UK's desire for access to EU markets and programs with its wish to maintain sovereignty in certain policy areas. It would involve ongoing negotiations to manage this complex relationship.

Scenario 3: Cooperative but Independent Entities

Strategic Partnerships

If the UK remains outside the EU, the relationship could evolve into one of strategic partnership, focusing on mutual interests like global security, climate change, and international trade. This scenario would see the UK and EU as cooperative but independent entities on the global stage.

Economic Realignment

In this scenario, the UK would continue to forge its independent trade policy while seeking to maintain a strong economic relationship with the EU. This could lead to a unique economic dynamic, balancing internal market access with global trade opportunities.

Scenario 4: Fluctuating Relations

Periodic Tensions and Alignments

Given the complex history and the impact of Brexit, the relationship between the UK and EU might be characterized by fluctuations, with periods of close alignment interspersed with tensions.

Political changes in either the UK or EU member states could significantly influence the nature of the relationship.

Diplomatic and Trade Challenges

This scenario would pose challenges in maintaining stable diplomatic and trade relations. It would require continuous efforts from both sides to manage disagreements and capitalize on periods of alignment for mutual benefit.

Long-Term Economic Implications

Trade and Market Dynamics

Long-term economic relations would be significantly influenced by the chosen scenario. Full reintegration would mean deep economic integration, while other scenarios would result in a more nuanced economic relationship, with varying levels of access to each other's markets.

Investment and Financial Services

The UK's position as a financial hub would be influenced by its relationship with the EU. Closer ties could bolster London's status, while a more independent stance might require the UK to diversify its financial services sector.

Political and Cultural Considerations

Shaping European and Global Policies

The UK's role in shaping European and global policies would depend on the depth of its relationship with the EU. Closer integration would offer more influence in European affairs, while a more independent stance could see the UK pursuing a distinct global role.

Identity and Perception

The long-term relationship will also impact cultural and social identities in the UK and EU. Full reintegration might strengthen a

European identity in the UK, while other scenarios could reinforce a more distinct British identity.

Conclusion

The long-term relationship between the UK and the EU post-Brexit reversal is subject to a range of potential scenarios, each with its implications and dynamics. The future could see anything from full reintegration to strategic but independent partnerships, with varying impacts on trade, politics, and culture. These scenarios underscore the complexities and possibilities inherent in this pivotal transnational relationship, highlighting the importance of strategic foresight and diplomatic agility in shaping a mutually beneficial future.

Potential Scenarios and Their Implications

The long-term relationship between the United Kingdom and the European Union post-Brexit is shrouded in potential scenarios, each carrying distinct implications for the future of both entities. This section explores these scenarios, analyzing their possible impacts on political, economic, and social landscapes.

Scenario 1: Full Reintegration with Enhanced Role

In this scenario, the UK not only rejoins the EU but also takes on a more active and influential role.

Implications:

- **Political Influence:** The UK could have greater influence in shaping EU policies, especially in areas like security, environment, and digital regulation.
- **Economic Integration:** Full access to the Single Market would likely boost the UK's economic growth, though it may require compliance with EU regulations that the UK previously opposed.

- **Social and Cultural Impact:** Enhanced freedom of movement could lead to a richer cultural exchange and more robust educational collaborations.

Scenario 2: Associate Membership Model

Here, the UK rejoins the EU but under an associate membership model, similar to Norway or Switzerland, with access to specific sectors like trade and research.

Implications:

- **Selective Market Access:** The UK would enjoy certain benefits of the Single Market without full membership, balancing national sovereignty with economic advantages.
- **Negotiation and Compromise:** This scenario would require continuous negotiation over access and contributions, potentially leading to periodic tensions.
- **Regulatory Challenges:** The UK would need to align with EU regulations in agreed sectors, which could cause friction in areas of divergence.

Scenario 3: Strategic Partnership

The UK and EU could form a strategic partnership, focusing on mutual interests without formal membership.

Implications:

- **Independent Trade Policies:** The UK would maintain more control over its trade policies but might lack the leverage that comes with EU membership.
- **Collaboration in Global Issues:** Joint efforts in addressing global challenges like climate change and security could be beneficial for both parties.
- **Cultural and Educational Ties:** While there might be fewer exchanges than full membership allows, targeted programs could sustain cultural and educational links.

Scenario 4: Competitive Coexistence

A scenario where the UK and EU evolve as competitive entities, each seeking to maximize their interests, sometimes at the expense of the other.

Implications:

- **Economic Competition:** This could lead to competition for trade deals, investments, and technological advancements.
- **Political Divergence:** Potential for divergent political stances on global issues, reducing the scope for collaboration.
- **Reduced Social and Cultural Exchange:** Less interaction could lead to a gradual weakening of social and cultural ties.

Scenario 5: Renewed Partnership with Limited Integration

In this scenario, the UK and EU re-establish a partnership based on limited integration, focusing on trade and security cooperation.

Implications:

- **Balanced Economic Relationship:** A pragmatic approach focusing on trade and investment could lead to a stable economic relationship.
- **Cooperation on Security:** Shared security concerns could foster close cooperation, benefiting both parties in tackling cross-border threats.
- **Preservation of Distinct Identities:** Limited integration allows both the UK and EU to maintain distinct political and cultural identities.

Scenario 6: Progressive Re-engagement

A gradual re-engagement scenario where the UK incrementally increases its alignment with the EU, potentially leading to full membership in the long run.

Implications:

- **Staged Economic Alignment:** A step-by-step approach to market access and regulatory alignment could minimize disruptions.
- **Phased Political Reintegration:** Gradual re-engagement could allow time to rebuild trust and adjust to new political realities.
- **Cultural and Social Reconnection:** Incremental re-engagement could foster a gradual strengthening of cultural and educational ties.

Conclusion

The future relationship between the UK and EU spans a spectrum of possibilities, each with unique implications. These scenarios range from full reintegration to more independent or competitive stances, influencing economic, political, and social dynamics. The chosen path will significantly shape the nature of trans-European cooperation and the global roles of both the UK and the EU. Navigating this landscape will require strategic foresight, diplomatic agility, and a keen understanding of the mutual and individual interests at play.

Conclusion

Summarizing Key Points

The discussion surrounding the potential reversal of Brexit and the UK's reintegration into the European Union is multifaceted, encompassing a range of legal, political, economic, and social dimensions. This section summarizes the key points explored in the preceding chapters, providing a cohesive overview of the complexities and considerations involved in this significant geopolitical topic.

The Historical Context and Impact of Brexit

Brexit, a monumental decision in the UK's history, has had far-reaching effects:

- **Economic Implications:** Brexit has impacted trade, investment, and the overall economic landscape of the UK, introducing new challenges and uncertainties.
- **Political Repercussions:** Domestically, Brexit has led to political realignments and debates about national sovereignty, while internationally, it has altered the UK's role on the global stage.
- **Social Consequences:** The decision has influenced social dynamics within the UK, affecting issues of identity, immigration, and cultural exchange.

The Case for and Against Reversal

The argument for reversing Brexit is multi-dimensional but faces significant counterarguments:

- **Economic Rationale:** Advocates for reversal emphasize potential economic stability and benefits from rejoining the EU, though opponents point to the risks of economic disruption and loss of newly formed global trade relationships.
- **Political and Legal Complexities:** The feasibility of reversing Brexit involves navigating complex legal procedures and political dynamics, both domestically and within the EU.

- **Social Considerations:** Reversal proponents highlight the potential social and cultural benefits of EU membership, while opponents express concerns about further societal polarization.

Legal and Political Mechanisms for Reversal

Reversing Brexit would require navigating a series of legal and political steps:

- **Legal Framework:** This involves domestic legal adjustments, formal application procedures, and negotiations with the EU.
- **Political Processes:** Achieving domestic consensus, engaging in diplomatic efforts with EU member states, and ensuring compliance with EU standards are key political challenges.

Economic, Diplomatic, and Social Implications

The economic, diplomatic, and social implications of a potential reversal are extensive:

- **Economic Outlook:** The impact on trade, financial services, and the labor market are pivotal considerations.
- **Diplomatic Dynamics:** Rejoining the EU would affect the UK's global diplomatic relationships and its role in addressing international challenges.
- **Social Impact:** Issues related to identity, cultural exchange, and freedom of movement are central to the social implications of reintegration.

Future Scenarios and Relationships

Looking ahead, various scenarios for the UK-EU relationship present unique implications:

- **Full Reintegration:** This scenario offers maximum economic and political integration but requires significant legal and social adjustments.

- **Partial Association or Strategic Partnership:** These options provide a balance between some benefits of EU membership and greater UK sovereignty.

- **Independent Coexistence:** A more distant relationship would preserve the UK's autonomy but might limit economic and diplomatic benefits.

Overcoming Challenges and Employing Strategies

Addressing the challenges of a potential reversal involves employing strategic approaches:

- **Engagement and Communication:** Transparent communication and public engagement are essential for building a democratic mandate.

- **Economic and Legal Planning:** Careful economic and legal planning can mitigate disruptions and align UK policies with EU standards.

- **Diplomatic Outreach:** Proactive diplomacy is necessary to rebuild trust and secure support from EU member states.

Conclusion

In sum, the prospect of reversing Brexit and rejoining the EU presents a complex array of considerations. From legal procedures and economic impacts to political dynamics and social implications, each aspect contributes to the overarching narrative of this significant geopolitical issue. While the feasibility and desirability of such a reversal are subjects of debate, understanding these multifaceted elements is crucial for any comprehensive discussion about the future relationship between the UK and the EU. Whether or not a reversal occurs, the dialogue surrounding this topic continues to shape the political, economic, and social landscapes of both the UK and Europe.

Final Thoughts on the Feasibility and Desirability of Reversing Brexit

As the United Kingdom navigates its post-Brexit reality, discussions around the feasibility and desirability of reversing this decision remain prevalent. This conclusion synthesizes the complexities of such a reversal, weighing the various factors that would influence its practicality and appeal.

Assessing the Feasibility of Reversal

Legal and Procedural Challenges

The legal and procedural route to reversing Brexit is fraught with complexities. It involves not only domestic legislative changes but also intricate negotiations with the European Union, requiring unanimous agreement among member states. The process would demand significant time, resources, and political capital.

Economic Considerations

From an economic perspective, the feasibility hinges on the UK's ability to reintegrate into the EU's market structures and regulatory frameworks. While rejoining could potentially stabilize trade and investment, it would also necessitate adjustments in newly established trade relationships outside the EU.

Political Dynamics

Politically, the feasibility depends on gaining a robust democratic mandate. This would likely require a new referendum or a decisive general election outcome, reflecting a clear shift in public opinion. Furthermore, it necessitates navigating the EU's willingness to readmit the UK under potentially renegotiated terms of membership.

Evaluating the Desirability of Reversal

Economic Benefits versus Sovereignty

The desirability of reversing Brexit is a balance between the economic benefits of EU membership and the value placed on national sovereignty. While rejoining the EU promises access to the Single Market and customs union, it also means adhering to EU regulations and policies, potentially limiting the UK's autonomy in certain areas.

Social and Cultural Implications

The social aspect of EU membership – particularly the free movement of people – has both supporters and detractors. While some view it as a means to enrich cultural and educational experiences, others are concerned about its impact on national identity and immigration control.

Global Standing and Influence

Rejoining the EU could enhance the UK's global influence by aligning with a powerful economic and political bloc. However, it could also be perceived as a retreat from the global ambitions signified by Brexit, impacting the UK's standing as an independent global player.

Potential Scenarios and Long-Term Outlook

Full Reintegration

A complete reversal and reintegration into the EU would likely bring the UK back into the core of European politics and economics. However, it could also reignite domestic divisions and raise questions about the UK's long-term commitment to the EU.

A New, Modified Relationship

An alternative scenario could involve negotiating a new form of association with the EU, distinct from full membership. This would aim to balance the benefits of economic integration with a greater degree of political independence.

Maintaining the Status Quo

Conversely, maintaining the current post-Brexit status could solidify the UK's position as an independent entity. While this upholds certain aspects of national sovereignty, it also means navigating the challenges of being outside the EU's structures.

Conclusion

The discussion around reversing Brexit entails a complex interplay of legal, economic, political, social, and global factors. Its feasibility is contingent on a myriad of procedural, diplomatic, and legislative hurdles, while its desirability is a subject of deep national reflection, balancing economic advantages against sovereignty and independence.

Ultimately, the decision to pursue or forego the reversal of Brexit is not just a technical or economic one; it is profoundly about the kind of future the UK envisions for itself both within Europe and on the global stage. It requires careful consideration of the UK's role in an increasingly interconnected world, its economic priorities, and the values and aspirations of its people. Whether the UK eventually gravitates back towards the EU or forges ahead on its independent path, the implications of this decision will resonate for generations to come, shaping the UK's identity, influence, and prosperity in the 21st century.

Appendix A: Relevant Legal Documents and Treaties

The legal framework governing the United Kingdom's membership in, exit from, and potential rejoining of the European Union is underpinned by a series of critical legal documents and treaties. This appendix provides an overview of these key documents, offering context and reference for understanding the legalities involved in the UK's relationship with the EU.

The Treaty on European Union (TEU)

Overview

The Treaty on European Union, often referred to as the Maastricht Treaty, is a foundational legal document for the EU. It sets out the principles and objectives of the Union, including the criteria and process for membership.

Relevance to Brexit

The TEU was central to the UK's membership in the EU and subsequently to the Brexit process. Article 50 of the TEU, which outlines the procedure for a member state to withdraw from the Union, was invoked by the UK to initiate Brexit.

The Treaty on the Functioning of the European Union (TFEU)

Overview

The TFEU complements the TEU and details the specific roles and functions of the EU's institutions. It also elaborates on EU policies, including the internal market, competition law, and other areas of EU competence.

Relevance to Brexit

The TFEU governed many aspects of the UK's obligations and rights as an EU member state, including participation in the Single Market and adherence to EU regulations.

The Lisbon Treaty

Overview

The Lisbon Treaty, which came into force in 2009, amended the TEU and TFEU. It enhanced the EU's decision-making process and increased the powers of the European Parliament.

Relevance to Brexit

The Lisbon Treaty's amendments to the TEU and TFEU impacted the legal framework within which Brexit negotiations and process-es took place.

The European Communities Act 1972

Overview

This was a key piece of UK legislation that facilitated the UK's acces-sion to the European Economic Community, which later became the EU. It made EU law directly applicable in the UK.

Relevance to Brexit

The European Communities Act 1972 was repealed by the European Union (Withdrawal) Act 2018, a critical legal step in formalizing Brexit.

The European Union (Withdrawal) Act 2018

Overview

This Act of the UK Parliament provided the legal framework for the UK's withdrawal from the EU. It repealed the European Communities Act 1972 and converted existing EU law into UK law.

Relevance to Brexit

The Act was essential in ensuring a functioning statute book following the UK's exit from the EU. It also set out the legal process for incorporating the Withdrawal Agreement into UK law.

The Withdrawal Agreement

Overview

The Withdrawal Agreement is a treaty negotiated between the UK and the EU that set out the terms of the UK's exit from the Union. It covers citizens' rights, the financial settlement, and other separation issues.

Relevance to Brexit

The Withdrawal Agreement was ratified by both the UK and the EU and laid down the conditions for the UK's withdrawal, including provisions for the transition period.

The Trade and Cooperation Agreement

Overview

Negotiated post-Brexit, this agreement outlines the future relationship between the UK and the EU. It covers trade in goods and services, digital trade, intellectual property, and law enforcement, among other areas.

Relevance to Post-Brexit Relations

The Trade and Cooperation Agreement governs the current economic and security relationship between the UK and the EU and would be a reference point for any discussions on rejoining the EU.

Conclusion

These documents collectively form the legal backbone of the UK's past and present relationship with the European Union. Understanding these treaties and acts is crucial for comprehensively grasping the legal intricacies of Brexit and any potential moves to reverse it. For policymakers, scholars, and citizens alike, these documents provide the essential legal context for navigating the complex terrain of UK-EU relations.

Appendix B: Economic Data and Analysis

This appendix provides an overview of pertinent economic data and analysis related to Brexit, offering a quantitative basis for understanding its impacts and the potential effects of a reversal. The data encompasses various economic indicators pre- and post-Brexit, shedding light on the UK's economic performance and its changing economic relationship with the European Union.

GDP Growth Rates

Pre- and Post-Brexit Trends

- **Pre-Brexit Period:** Prior to Brexit, the UK's GDP growth rate was generally aligned with the broader EU average.
- **Post-Brexit Impact:** Following the Brexit referendum and subsequent negotiations, a slowdown in GDP growth was observed, attributed to uncertainties and changes in trade dynamics.

Trade Volumes and Patterns

Shifts in Import and Export Dynamics

- **EU Trade:** The UK's trade with the EU, historically its largest trading partner, experienced shifts post-Brexit, with a notable decrease in certain sectors due to new trade barriers.
- **Global Trade:** Post-Brexit, the UK has been actively pursuing and establishing new trade agreements outside the EU, though these are yet to fully compensate for the loss of frictionless EU trade.

Foreign Direct Investment (FDI)

Changes in Investment Flows

- **Pre-Brexit Levels:** The UK was one of the leading recipients of FDI in Europe, attributed to its access to the EU Single Market.
- **Post-Brexit Trends:** There has been a marked decline in FDI inflows post-Brexit, reflecting investor uncertainty regarding the UK's future economic landscape.

Unemployment Rates

Labor Market Impacts

- **Historical Data:** The UK's unemployment rate pre-Brexit was comparatively low within the EU context.
- **Post-Brexit Scenario:** While unemployment rates have remained relatively stable, there are concerns about labor shortages in certain sectors, partly due to changes in immigration rules.

Inflation Rates

Consumer Prices and Cost of Living

- **Trends over Time:** Inflation rates in the UK have shown fluctuations post-Brexit, influenced by the depreciation of the pound and changes in import costs.
- **Comparative Analysis:** When compared to the EU average, the UK's inflation rate has exhibited differing trends, impacted by distinct national policies and external economic factors.

Sector-Specific Impacts

Analysis by Industry

- **Manufacturing and Agriculture:** These sectors have faced significant challenges due to new trade barriers and loss of subsidies like the EU's Common Agricultural Policy.

- **Services Sector:** As a major component of the UK economy, the services sector, particularly financial services, has been impacted by the loss of passporting rights and uncertainties about market access.

Public Finances

Government Revenue and Expenditure

- **Budget Contributions and Receipts:** Analysis of the UK's contributions to and receipts from the EU budget pre-Brexit.
- **Post-Brexit Fiscal Changes:** Changes in public finances post-Brexit, including adjustments in government spending and revenue patterns.

Consumer Market Changes

Retail and Consumer Behavior

- **Consumer Confidence:** Trends in consumer confidence pre- and post-Brexit, reflecting economic sentiments.
- **Retail Sales:** Data on retail sales, providing insights into consumer spending and economic activity.

Economic Projections and Scenarios

Forecasting Future Trends

- **Short-term Forecasts:** Economic projections for the next few years, considering factors like trade deals, fiscal policies, and global economic conditions.
- **Long-term Outlook:** Scenarios for the UK's economic future in the context of its evolving relationship with the EU and global economic trends.

Conclusion

This economic data and analysis provide a factual foundation for assessing the impacts of Brexit and the potential repercussions of a reversal. The indicators highlight shifts in trade, investment, labor market dynamics, public finances, and consumer behavior, offering a comprehensive view of the UK's economic trajectory in relation to its changing relationship with the European Union. For policy-makers, businesses, and researchers, this information is crucial for informed decision-making and strategic planning in the context of the UK's economic future.

Appendix C: Public Opinion Polls

Public opinion polls play a critical role in gauging the sentiment of the populace on key issues, including Brexit and the prospect of its reversal. This appendix collates and analyzes various public opinion polls conducted before and after the Brexit referendum, providing insight into how public attitudes have evolved over time.

Pre-Brexit Referendum Polls

Trends Leading to the 2016 Vote

- **2015-2016 Polls:** In the lead-up to the Brexit referendum, polls showed a divided nation, with a narrow margin between Leave and Remain supporters. These polls reflected key concerns such as sovereignty, immigration, and economic prospects.
- **Influencing Factors:** Analysis of these polls indicates that voter sentiment was influenced by factors including demographic variables (age, education level, region), political affiliation, and socio-economic status.

Post-Brexit Referendum Polls

Immediate Aftermath

- **2016-2017 Polls:** Immediately following the referendum, polls suggested a slight shift in opinion, with some voters expressing regret (termed "Bregret"), while others remained steadfast in their decision.
- **Key Concerns:** Post-referendum polls highlighted concerns about the economic impact of Brexit, the complexities of the withdrawal process, and the implications for UK unity.

Post-Brexit Transition Period Polls

Evolving Public Opinion

- **2018-2020 Polls:** During the transition period, polls reflected growing concerns about the practicalities of Brexit, with increasing focus on trade negotiations, the Irish border issue, and the rights of EU citizens in the UK and vice versa.

- **Shifts in Sentiment:** Some polls indicated a gradual shift towards a more favorable view of the EU, particularly among younger voters and those affected by Brexit's economic implications.

Current Public Opinion Polls

Recent Trends and Opinions

- **2021-Onward Polls:** Recent polls suggest a complex picture, with some segments of the population showing increasing skepticism about the benefits of Brexit, while others remain convinced of its merits.

- **Factors Influencing Current Sentiment:** Ongoing trade issues, the economic impact of Brexit combined with global challenges such as the COVID-19 pandemic, and political changes within the UK and EU are influencing current public opinion.

Regional Variations in Public Opinion

Differences Across the UK

- **England, Scotland, Wales, Northern Ireland:** Polls indicate significant regional variations in attitudes towards Brexit and its potential reversal. Scotland and Northern Ireland, which voted predominantly to remain, have consistently shown higher support for rejoining the EU compared to England and Wales.

- **Regional Economic and Political Factors:** These variations are influenced by regional economic dependencies on the EU, political representation, and cultural ties to Europe.

Demographic Differences in Brexit Opinions

Age, Education, and Socio-Economic Status

- **Age-Related Trends:** Younger voters, particularly those who have come of age post-referendum, tend to be more pro-EU, as reflected in recent polls.
- **Impact of Education and Socio-Economic Status:** Higher education levels and socio-economic status are correlated with a preference for remaining in or rejoining the EU, highlighting the role of economic prospects and cultural exposure in shaping Brexit opinions.

Public Opinion on Specific Brexit Issues

Views on Trade, Immigration, and Sovereignty

- **Trade and Economic Impacts:** Polls consistently show that trade and economic issues are key concerns for the public, with varying opinions on whether Brexit has improved or hindered the UK's economic position.
- **Immigration and Sovereignty:** While immigration was a significant factor in the pre-referendum polls, its prominence has varied in recent years, with more focus shifting to issues of national sovereignty and global influence.

Conclusion

The analysis of public opinion polls from before and after the Brexit referendum provides valuable insights into the evolving perspectives of the UK population. These polls reflect a dynamic and often divided public sentiment, influenced by a range of economic, political, and social factors. Understanding these trends is crucial for policymakers, analysts, and scholars in assessing the current state of public opinion and in anticipating potential shifts in the future.

As the UK navigates its post-Brexit landscape, these polls offer a critical barometer of the public mood and preferences regarding the UK's relationship with the EU.

Further Reading Materials

This bibliography provides a curated list of references and further reading materials that offer deeper insights into the topics covered in the discussion of Brexit, its implications, and the potential for its reversal. These resources range from academic texts and official documents to insightful analyses and commentaries, providing a comprehensive understanding of the multifaceted nature of Brexit.

Foundational Legal Texts

1. Treaty on European Union (TEU)

- Essential for understanding the legal framework of the EU and the provisions for membership and withdrawal.

2. Treaty on the Functioning of the European Union (TFEU)

- Provides detailed insights into the functioning and policies of the EU.

3. The Lisbon Treaty

- Offers a perspective on the amendments to the TEU and TFEU, impacting the UK's relationship with the EU.

4. The European Union (Withdrawal) Act 2018

- Key legal document for understanding the UK's legislative process in withdrawing from the EU.

Economic Analysis and Data

1. "The Economic Consequences of Brexit: A Taxing Decision," OECD Economic Policy Papers

   - Analyzes the economic impact of Brexit on the UK and the broader EU economy.

2. "Brexit: The Economics of International Disintegration," by Swati Dhingra and Thomas Sampson

   - Offers an in-depth analysis of the economic implications of Brexit.

3. UK Office for National Statistics (ONS) Reports

   - Provides statistical data on the UK's economic performance pre- and post-Brexit.

Political and Social Perspectives

1. "Brexitland: Identity, Diversity and the Reshaping of British Politics," by Maria Sobolewska and Robert Ford

   - Explores the social and political factors that shaped the Brexit vote and its aftermath.

2. "The Road to Somewhere: The Populist Revolt and the Future of Politics," by David Goodhart

   - Provides insights into the cultural and political divides revealed by the Brexit referendum.

International Relations and Diplomacy

1. "Brexit and British Foreign Policy," by David Allen and Tim Oliver

   - Discusses the implications of Brexit on the UK's foreign policy and international relations.

2. "The European Union's External Action and International Law," by Piet Eeckhout and Manuel López-Escudero

- Useful for understanding the EU's international legal framework, relevant to the UK's negotiations for rejoining.

Case Studies and Comparative Analyses

1. "The European Union and Member State Territories: A New Legal Framework Under the EU Treaties," by Fiona Murray

- Offers comparative case studies of other regions' experiences with EU membership and withdrawal.

2. "The Politics of European Integration," by Michael O'Neill

- Provides broader context and comparisons with other EU integration and disintegration processes.

Brexit Reversal: Theoretical and Practical Considerations

1. "Can Brexit Be Reversed? The Legal and Political Considerations," by Catherine Barnard

- Examines the legal and political aspects of potentially reversing Brexit.

2. "Brexit and the Future of the European Union: The Case for Constitutional Reforms," by Federico Fabbrini

- Discusses potential reforms in the EU that could impact the feasibility and desirability of the UK rejoining.

Public Opinion and Surveys

1. British Election Study Reports

- Provides insights into public opinion trends and shifts regarding Brexit and related issues.

2. Eurobarometer Surveys

- Offers data on European public opinion, including perceptions of Brexit and its implications.

Conclusion

This bibliography serves as a foundation for those seeking to delve deeper into the complexities of Brexit and the multifaceted considerations surrounding its potential reversal. These resources provide valuable perspectives and analyses, aiding in a comprehensive understanding of the legal, economic, political, and social dimensions of this pivotal issue in contemporary European and global affairs.